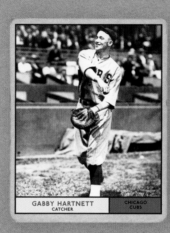

GABBY HARTNETT
CATCHER

CHICAGO
CUBS

ERNIE BANKS
SHORTSTOP

CHICAGO
CUBS

THE STORY OF THE CHICAGO CUBS

Published by Creative Education
P.O. Box 227, Mankato, Minnesota 56002
Creative Education is an imprint of The Creative Company
www.thecreativecompany.us

Design and production by Blue Design
Art direction by Rita Marshall
Printed by Corporate Graphics in the United States of America

Photographs by Getty Images (Lee Balterman/Time & Life Pictures, Bernstein Associates, Jonathan Daniel, Elsa, Michele Falzone, G. Flume, Chris McGrath, Ronald C. Modra/Sports Imagery, National Baseball Hall of Fame Library/MLB Photos, Photo File/MLB Photos, Rich Pilling/MLB Photos, Louis Requena/MLB Photos, Mark Rucker/Transcendental Graphics, Jamie Squire, Scott Strazzate/Chicago Tribune/MCT, Stock Montage, Chris Trotman, Ron Vesely/MLB Photos)

Library of Congress Cataloging-in-Publication Data

Gilbert, Sara.
The story of the Chicago Cubs / by Sara Gilbert.
p. cm. — (Baseball: the great American game)
Includes index.
Summary: The history of the Chicago Cubs professional baseball team from its inaugural 1876 season to today, spotlighting the team's greatest players and most memorable moments.
ISBN 978-1-60818-035-6
1. Chicago Cubs (Baseball team)—History—Juvenile literature. I. Title. II. Series.

GV875.C6G55 2011
796.357'640977311—dc22   2010023567

CPSIA: 110310 PO1381

First Edition
9 8 7 6 5 4 3 2 1

Page 3: *First baseman Cap Anson*
Page 4: *Left fielder Alfonso Soriano*

BASEBALL: THE GREAT AMERICAN GAME

THE STORY OF THE CHICAGO CUBS

Sara Gilbert

CREATIVE EDUCATION

CONTENTS

THE CUBS ARE BORN

Chicago, Illinois, has been known as the "Windy City" since the late 1800s. Some suggest that the nickname took root because the city, which was built on the banks of Lake Michigan in the early 1800s, is often visited by fierce breezes off the lake. Some say it was born out of a rivalry with the city of Cincinnati, Ohio, which used the nickname derisively, or that a New York City newspaperman coined the term when Chicago hosted the World's Fair in 1893. Still others claim that it's a reference to how eager many of Chicago's 2.8 million residents are to brag about their midwestern home.

Those residents, who make Chicago the third-largest metropolitan area in the United States, can take pride in many things about their city—including the fact that Chicago boasts professional teams in every prominent American sport, including one of the oldest major league baseball clubs in the country: the Chicago Cubs. When baseball's National League (NL) was founded in 1876, the Chicago White Stockings, whose name later changed to the Cubs, were one of the original teams.

Downtown Chicago has long been marked by towering skyscrapers, including the 108-story Willis Tower (named the Sears Tower until 2009).

PITCHER · MORDECAI BROWN

When a boy grows up with a nickname like "Three Finger," his prospects of becoming a major-league pitcher are not great. As a child, Mordecai Brown lost a finger in a farm machine accident. Later, while chasing a rabbit, he fell and broke his other fingers, leaving him with a bent middle finger, a paralyzed pinky, and a mere stump of an index finger. This odd combination, however, allowed him to get a grip on a baseball that provided excellent movement, much like the split-finger fastball thrown by pitchers today. Brown pitched 10 years for the Cubs, posting 6 consecutive seasons of 20 or more victories.

MORDECAI BROWN
PITCHER

CHICAGO CUBS

STATS

Cubs seasons: 1904–12, 1916

Height: 5-foot-10

Weight: 175

- **239–130 career record**

- **271 complete games**

- **2.06 career ERA**

- **Baseball Hall of Fame inductee (1949)**

Player/manager A. G. Spalding pitched the team's first game and recorded its first hit on April 25 of that year, launching a 52–14 campaign that earned Chicago the league's first pennant. But after the team posted a losing record in 1877, Spalding retired. In 1879, first baseman Adrian "Cap" Anson began a 19-year tenure as the team's manager, leading Chicago to 5 NL pennants by 1886. But in the next decade, the team slipped low in the standings, where it would remain until the turn of the century.

During the early years of professional baseball, it was common for a team to change its name frequently. The Chicago squad was known by 15 different names during its first 25 years, from White Stockings to Colts and even Orphans. But when the club went through an obvious youth movement in 1902 under the leadership of new manager Frank Selee, a Chicago newspaper began to refer to the young team as the "Cubs." By 1903, the team had adopted the title as its official name.

The early years of the 1900s were golden ones for Cubs baseball. In 1907, another player/manager, first baseman Frank Chance, led the Cubs to their first World Series victory as they beat the Detroit Tigers and star outfielder Ty Cobb. The Cubs won the world championship

again in 1908 behind the pitching of Mordecai "Three Finger" Brown and the most famous double-play trio in history: shortstop Joe Tinker, second baseman Johnny Evers, and Chance. Franklin Pierce Adams, a writer for the *New York Evening Mail*, wrote of the Cubs' outstanding infield in poetic form after a matchup between Chicago and the New York Giants in July 1910: "Making a Giant hit into a double — / Words that are weighty with nothing but trouble: / Tinker to Evers to Chance."

The second decade of the 20th century continued where the previous had left off. The Cubs' power-hitting lineup punched Chicago's ticket to the World Series twice, the first time in 1910. The team came up short that year, losing to the Philadelphia Athletics four games to one. The seasons that followed were mostly unspectacular but not without their highlights. In one June 1911 game, second baseman Heinie Zimmerman slugged a team-record 9 runs batted in (RBI) during a 20–2 rout of the Boston Red Sox. In 1918, the Cubs reached the World Series again but fell four games to two, this time to the Red Sox in a tight, low-scoring affair.

Famed Cubs infielders Joe Tinker, Johnny Evers, and Frank Chance (pictured left to right) turned double plays together from 1902 to 1912.

A SCORCHING START

The National Association of Professional Baseball Players was founded in early 1871, with the Chicago White Stockings—an early name for the team that would later become the Cubs—as one of the league's inaugural members. The White Stockings made a good showing in the young league by remaining contenders over much of that first summer, but adversity hit in early October. On October 8, 1871, the Great Chicago Fire (allegedly started when a cow kicked over a lantern in a barn) ravaged the city. The fire devastated an area covering more than 2,000 acres and, in the process, destroyed the White Stockings' ballpark, uniforms, and other equipment. The club was forced to finish its schedule playing in borrowed uniforms. Despite such setbacks, the White Stockings finished second in the standings, trailing the Philadelphia Athletics by just two games. The havoc caused by the fire forced the team to drop out of the league while Chicago rebuilt from the ashes, but the White Stockings were revived in 1874. By 1876, the National Association gave way to the newly formed National League, and the Cubs have been part of that league ever since.

CUBS

CATCHER · # GABBY HARTNETT

His teammates nicknamed quiet and polite Charles Hartnett "Gabby" during his rookie year, and the ironic moniker stuck with the hardworking catcher for the rest of his career. Not only is Hartnett considered the best catcher in Cubs history, but he was commonly regarded as the best catcher in the NL before Cincinnati Reds great Johnny Bench put on the mask in 1967. A late bloomer, Hartnett hit his stride as he entered his 30s. From 1930 to 1937, he caught at least 116 games each year, and in 1939, he broke the big-league record of 1,727 career games behind the plate.

STATS

Cubs seasons: 1922–40

Height: 6-foot-1

Weight: 195

- .297 career BA

- 6-time All-Star

- 1935 NL MVP

- Baseball Hall of Fame inductee (1955)

GABBY HARTNETT
CATCHER

CHICAGO
CUBS

FIRST BASEMAN · MARK GRACE

Mark Grace embodied the blue-collar spirit of Chicago. Never as flashy as home-run-bashing teammates such as Sammy Sosa and Andre Dawson, Grace was a consistent, steady, line-drive hitter who quietly compiled more hits and more doubles than any other batter in the major leagues between 1990 and 1999. Although the media spotlight was often directed at the long-ball hitters, the Chicago faithful loved Grace for his consistency and spirited personality. His dry humor, sure fielding, and steady contributions in the middle of the Cubs' lineup made him a favorite in both the clubhouse and the stands.

MARK GRACE
FIRST BASEMAN

CHICAGO
CUBS

STATS

Cubs seasons: 1988–2000

Height: 6-foot-2

Weight: 190

- .303 career BA

- 4-time Gold Glove winner

- 3-time All-Star

- 2,445 career hits

A HAPPY HOME

n 1916, the Cubs were purchased by Charles Weeghman, a former team owner in the ill-fated and independent Federal League, which was formed in 1914 to compete with the already established American and National Leagues. When it folded after the 1915 season, Weeghman bought the Cubs and moved the club to the north side of Chicago and into what would become one of the most celebrated stadiums in baseball, a place then known as Weeghman Park. In 1920, its name changed to Cubs Park, and in 1926, it was renamed once again in honor of new Cubs majority owner William Wrigley Jr.

Wrigley Field, known as "The Friendly Confines" because of its cozy dimensions and lively atmosphere, is still home to the Cubs today. Built in 1914, it is the second-oldest ballpark still in use in Major League Baseball, behind only Boston's Fenway Park, which opened in 1912. The ivy-covered outfield wall, classic marquee sign, and old-fashioned scoreboard make Wrigley Field a piece of baseball history that is adored by fans and players alike. Ernie Banks, a star shortstop for the Cubs in the 1950s and '60s, once praised its neighborhood atmosphere, saying, "Wrigley is like another home in the community. When you're in Wrigley, it's like you're visiting the family of all the people that live around here."

Despite their happy home, the Cubs managed only one first-place finish during the 1920s. The team finished first in the eight-team NL in 1932, 1935, and 1938 but failed miserably in the World Series each year—of the 14 total games played in all 3 series, the Cubs won just 2.

Even though they were never quite able to win it all, the Cubs gave the Wrigley faithful plenty to remember—and some things to regret—during this era. In 1930, center fielder Hack Wilson put together one of the most remarkable seasons ever at the plate, batting .356, clouting 56 home runs, and driving in 191 runs. In 1932, New York Yankees great Babe Ruth hit his famous "Called Shot" in Game 3 of the World Series versus the Cubs. And in the heat of the 1938 pennant race, catcher Gabby Hartnett hit a late home run in the near darkness of Wrigley Field, which didn't have lights yet, to help the Cubs clinch the pennant—a shot that earned a place in baseball lore as "The Homer in the Gloamin'."

In 1945, the Cubs made it to the World Series once again, only to

HACK WILSON

With his cartoonishly muscular physique and swing-for-the-fences approach, Hack Wilson kept fans riveted during his at bats in the late 1920s.

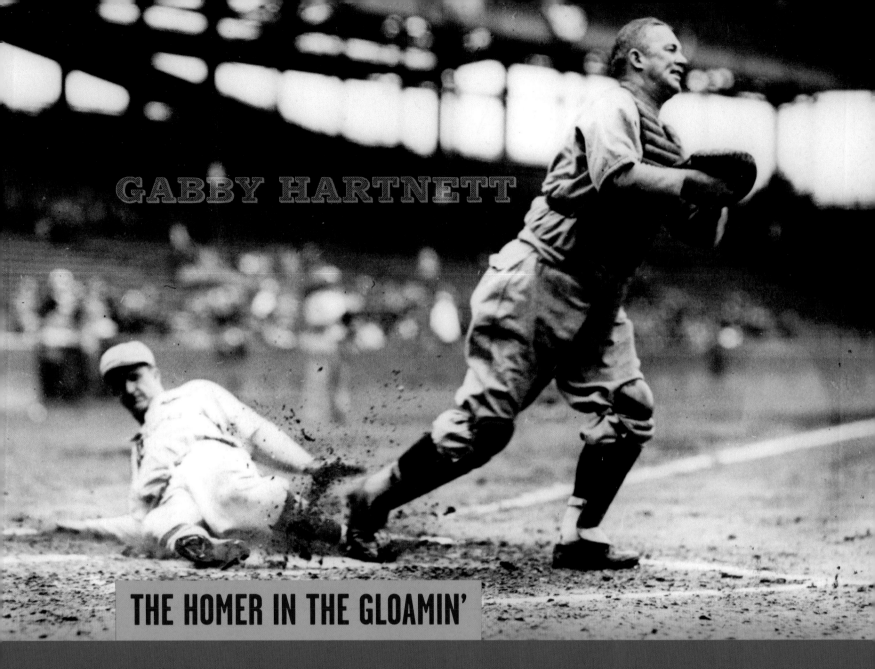

GABBY HARTNETT

THE HOMER IN THE GLOAMIN'

After star catcher Gabby Hartnett was named the Cubs' manager midway through the 1938 season, he engaged his team in a race with the Pittsburgh Pirates for the NL pennant. On September 28, the Pirates came to Chicago with a half-game lead over the hometown Cubs. Because Wrigley Field did not have lights yet, games were played during the daytime. This game, which had started in the afternoon, entered the ninth inning in a 5–5 tie. With two outs in the bottom of the ninth, the score remained deadlocked as darkness began to settle over Wrigley Field. Realizing that the umpires would call the game on account of darkness after the inning, Hartnett stepped to the plate hoping to finish the contest quickly. Although he couldn't really see through the fading light, he took a mighty swing where he hoped the pitch would be and connected, sending the ball screaming through the evening sky and over the fence. To this day, Hartnett's unlikely shot is known as "The Homer in the Gloamin'." That famous swing gave Chicago the lead over Pittsburgh in the pennant race, and the Cubs clinched the NL title three days later to reach their ninth World Series.

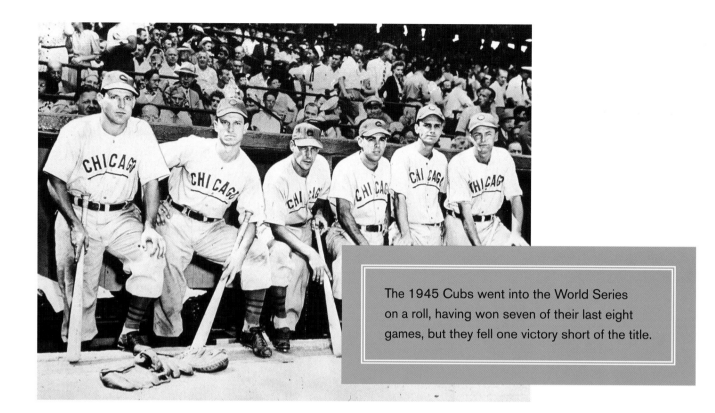

The 1945 Cubs went into the World Series on a roll, having won seven of their last eight games, but they fell one victory short of the title.

be foiled by the Tigers—and a goat named Senovia—in a seven-game series. Although Detroit and hard-hitting first baseman Hank Greenberg beat the Cubs fairly, four games to three, many fans blamed the loss on Senovia, who was banned from the ballpark by Cubs officials.

Chicagoan Billy Sianis had brought his goat to Wrigley Field for Game 4 as a good luck omen for his hometown team, but owner Phil Wrigley told him that Senovia was too stinky to be in the stadium. The story goes that Sianis angrily uttered a curse as he left the ballpark, saying that the Cubs, who had played in 10 World Series between 1900 and 1945, would never play in baseball's "Fall Classic" again. Few people considered those hastily spoken words a serious threat at the time, but little did they know.

CROSSTOWN RIVALS

By 1900, the Chicago Cubs were well established on the north side of Chicago. So when a new American League team, the White Sox, decided to put down roots, Cubs owners insisted that they stay on the south side. But starting in 1903, the Cubs and the White Sox began crossing those boundaries for a contest that became known as the "City Series." The first City Series ended with the two teams tied at seven wins apiece after the deciding 15th game was cancelled due to bad weather. When the last City Series ended in 1942, the Cubs had won the series only 6 times in 39 years. The rivalry picked up again in the 1980s, when the two teams began playing each other in an exhibition game once each season, often on Memorial Day. Although the "Windy City Classic," as it was called, didn't count toward either team's season record, it was a favorite with fans. In 1997, when Major League Baseball instituted interleague play, the White Sox and Cubs started playing each other six times a season. Those games have become some of the most anticipated and best-attended games of the year for Cubs and Sox fans.

CURSED CUBS

hat curse ended up weighing heavily on Cubs fans over the next few decades, as the team gave them little to get excited about in terms of wins and championships. Chicago missed the playoffs year after year, even though its lineup featured a number of outstanding players. It was bittersweet to see great players don Cubs uniforms because they were doomed, it seemed, to never experience the postseason.

"Sweet Swingin'" Billy Williams, a dangerous hitter and dependable left fielder, and Ron Santo, a fiery third baseman, were among those who made their names in Cubs blue during the 1960s and '70s. Under outspoken manager Leo Durocher, slick-fielding shortstop Don Kessinger and talented pitchers Dick Ellsworth and Ken Holtzman won many games for the Cubs but likewise fell short of October baseball. Fan favorite Ernie Banks, known as "Mr. Cub," also starred during this era, carving out a legendary career but never playing for a league or world championship. Yet true to his upbeat nature, the Hall of Fame shortstop looked for the silver lining in the Cubs' drought,

SECOND BASEMAN · RYNE SANDBERG

Ryne Sandberg, known simply as "Ryno" to the baseball world, was a natural talent who played several positions before taking over second base for the Cubs in 1982, where he stayed for most of his 15 years with the team. Ryno was a quiet team leader who once put together a streak of 123 straight games without a fielding error. His career numbers placed him among the Cubs' all-time leaders in nearly every major batting category. After announcing his retirement in 1994, Sandberg came back to play two more years in 1996 and 1997. He stayed connected to the franchise by becoming the manager of the Iowa Cubs, a Cubs minor-league affiliate, in 2010.

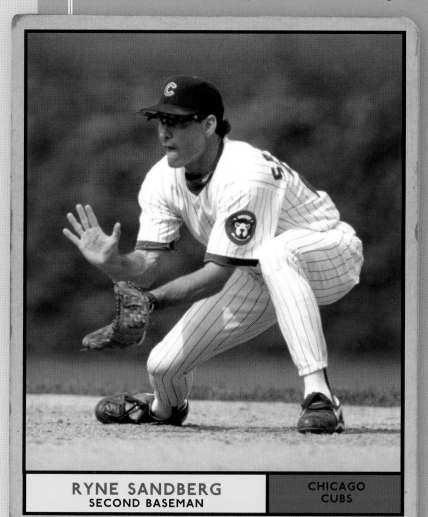

RYNE SANDBERG
SECOND BASEMAN

CHICAGO
CUBS

STATS

Cubs seasons: 1982–94, 1996–97

Height: 6-foot-1

Weight: 180

- **1984 NL MVP**

- **10-time All-Star**

- **9-time Gold Glove winner**

- **Baseball Hall of Fame inductee (2005)**

THIRD BASEMAN · RON SANTO

Some players wear their emotions on their sleeves, and Ron Santo was one of them. A feisty standout for the Cubs during the 1960s and early '70s, Santo was a great all-around third-sacker, winning five Gold Glove awards for his fielding prowess and hitting for both average and power. He also delighted Cubs fans by ritually clicking his heels in a celebratory dance each time the team won during the Cubs' run for the pennant in 1969. After his playing days ended, Santo embarked on a career in the radio booth as an analyst for Chicago.

RON SANTO
THIRD BASEMAN

CHICAGO
CUBS

STATS

Cubs seasons: 1960–73

Height: 6 feet

Weight: 190

- **9-time All-Star**

- **342 career HR**

- **2,254 career hits**

- **.277 career BA**

FERGIE JENKINS

once remarking, "The only way to prove you're a good sport is to lose."

Another Cubs great, fireball-throwing pitcher Fergie Jenkins, also shone during the team's prolonged slump. Regarded as one of the greatest African American pitchers in the history of the game, Jenkins won at least 20 games a season every year from 1967 to 1972. During each of those seasons, he managed to throw at least 20 complete games as well. Over a 10-year span, Jenkins won 167 games for a team that never finished better than second in its league or division (the NL was split into Eastern and Western divisions in 1969, with the Cubs placed in the NL East).

Banks retired in 1971, and by 1973, Jenkins was gone as well. Pitcher Bruce Sutter and outfielder Dave Kingman provided some highlights during the late '70s, but by the start of the 1981 season, the Cubs had missed the playoffs for 35 consecutive seasons. Even the most ardent fans began to wonder if the "Curse of the Billy Goat" held some

CUBS

truth to it after all, but Chicago crowds assembled regardless of their team's record. The Cubs' home attendance numbers remained among baseball's best, even as frustration set in.

In the early 1980s, Cubs fans celebrated some old heroes. In 1982, the team honored Ernie Banks by making his number 14 the first to be retired by the organization. That same season, Jenkins came back to pitch 2 more years after spending 8 seasons elsewhere and rang up his 3,000th career strikeout before hanging up his cleats in 1983.

The club also came under new leadership and found new stars during those years. The Wrigley family, who had owned the team since 1919, sold the Cubs to the Tribune Company (owner of the *Chicago Tribune* newspaper) for $20.5 million in 1981. And when the team added such talented young newcomers as outfielder Leon Durham and second baseman Ryne Sandberg, Chicago had good reason to hope the curse was about to end.

In 1984, behind the tremendous pitching of burly right-hander Rick Sutcliffe—who put up a 16–1 mark and won the Cy Young Award as the league's best pitcher—the Cubs won the NL East and made it to the playoffs for the first time since Billy Sianis had uttered his now-infamous oath in 1945. Sandberg exploded onto the scene in 1984 as

Ryne Sandberg came up through the Philadelphia Phillies' minor-league system before moving to the Windy City and becoming a star. The Cubs intended to make him an outfielder before he demonstrated his superb fielding at second base.

SHORTSTOP · ERNIE BANKS

In the long and colorful history of the Chicago Cubs, perhaps no player was as beloved as Ernie "Mr. Cub" Banks. Known for his constantly cheerful disposition, Banks enjoyed the game so much that his favorite phrase, rain or shine, was "It's a beautiful day for baseball." When he joined the team in 1953, Banks became the Cubs' first black player. Although he actually played more games at first base than at any other position, Banks will always be remembered as an energetic shortstop who hit for far more power than his lean frame suggested was possible. His number (14) became the first retired by the Cubs.

ERNIE BANKS
SHORTSTOP

CHICAGO
CUBS

STATS

Cubs seasons: 1953–71

Height: 6-foot-1

Weight: 180

- 512 career HR

- 2-time NL MVP

- 11-time All-Star

- Baseball Hall of Fame inductee (1977)

well, batting .314 and stealing 32 bases. Durham, fellow outfielders Gary Matthews and Keith Moreland, and third baseman Ron Cey all put together solid seasons, too, helping the team finish 96–65 and meet the San Diego Padres in the NL Championship Series (NLCS). But after winning the first two games, the Cubs dropped three in a row to the Padres and missed a berth in the World Series.

BACK IN THE HUNT

Sandberg continued to charm Chicago fans with his movie-star looks, solid fielding, and powerful bat, but the Cubs slid back down the standings for several seasons. In 1987, the team signed slugging right fielder Andre "The Hawk" Dawson. In his first season with the team, The Hawk belted 49 home runs to win the NL Most Valuable Player (MVP) award. Even Sandberg was left in awe of Dawson's amazing season, later saying, "I watched him win an MVP for a last-place team in 1987, and it was the most unbelievable thing I've ever seen in baseball."

By 1989, Chicago was again poised to make a playoff run. Along

LEFT FIELDER · BILLY WILLIAMS

"Sweet Swingin'" Billy Williams was a constant presence in left field for the Cubs from the early 1960s to the mid-1970s, setting an NL record with 1,117 consecutive games played. Williams is considered by many people to be one of the most overlooked stars of his time. He lacked the flash of teammates Ron Santo or Ernie Banks, yet he consistently put up outstanding statistics, stringing together 13 straight seasons with at least 20 home runs and 84 RBI. Williams never got the chance to play in a World Series, but his stellar career earned him a spot in the Baseball Hall of Fame in 1987.

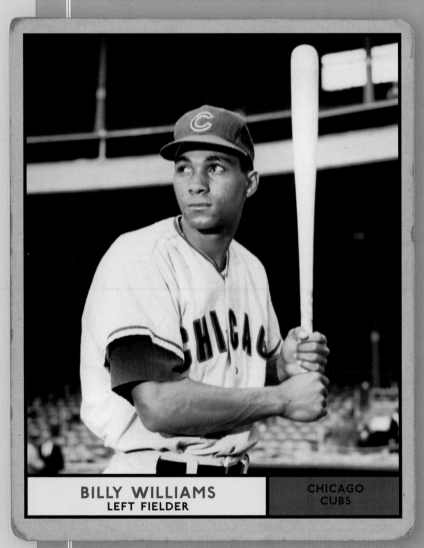

BILLY WILLIAMS
LEFT FIELDER

CHICAGO
CUBS

STATS

Cubs seasons: 1959–74

Height: 6-foot-1

Weight: 175

- **1961 NL Rookie of the Year**

- **6-time All-Star**

- **.290 career BA**

- **426 career HR**

LIGHTS AT WRIGLEY

The Cubs stood as a symbol of a baseball era gone by as they refused for many years to install lights at Wrigley Field. In fact, all Cubs home games were day games for the first 111 years of the club's history. Although it wasn't until 1988 that lights were added to Wrigley, that wasn't the first time that lights had been purchased for the stadium. Team president Phil Wrigley originally purchased a lighting system for Wrigley Field in the fall of 1941. However, after the bombing of Pearl Harbor on December 7, Wrigley donated the lights to the war effort. After the war, residents in the neighborhoods surrounding Wrigley Field opposed the addition of lights and nighttime games, and Wrigley himself preferred to keep the daytime schedule. It wasn't until the club was sold to the Tribune Company in 1981 that the daytime-only tradition was pushed aside in favor of a more fan-friendly schedule, and lights were installed. Although public opinion was largely split on the issue, team ownership threatened to move the Cubs if night games could not be a part of the schedule. The very first complete game under lights at Wrigley Field was played on August 9, 1988, as the Cubs defeated the New York Mets 6–4.

SAMMY SOSA

with Dawson and Sandberg, the Cubs featured emerging talents such as strong-armed shortstop Shawon Dunston and line-drive-hitting outfielder Jerome Walton, who won the NL Rookie of the Year award that season. The 1989 Cubs went 93–69 and won the NL East again, but they again lost in the NLCS, this time to the San Francisco Giants. Cubs first baseman Mark Grace made headlines by going 11-for-17 with 8 RBI in the NLCS, but it wasn't enough.

Dawson left town in 1992 but was replaced by a young slugger named Sammy Sosa. A native of the Dominican Republic, Sosa combined the youthful enthusiasm of Ernie Banks with the raw power of Hack Wilson, and scouts had immediately taken note of his lightning-quick bat and potential for power. Sosa was originally signed by the Texas Rangers in 1985 for a minimal $3,500 bonus; by 1998, he was making so much money with the Cubs that among the many cars he owned was a Rolls-Royce.

Still, it wasn't until the pitching staff improved in 1998 that the Cubs returned to the playoff scene and became a point of national interest. The club's pitching rotation that season featured the powerful arm of rookie Kerry Wood. Wood threw a fastball that consistently topped 95 miles per hour, and he took the league by storm despite being just

20 years old. In only his fifth start, he threw a one-hitter against the Houston Astros, striking out 20 batters to tie a big-league record set by all-time great Nolan Ryan. Wood went on to accumulate a 13–6 record, although a tender elbow sidelined him toward the end of the Cubs' run to the postseason.

While Wood was fanning opposing batters, Sosa was captivating the sports world as he engaged brawny St. Louis Cardinals first baseman Mark McGwire in a contest to beat Yankees outfielder Roger Maris's single-season home run mark of 61. The two sluggers were neck-and-neck for the majority of the season, but in the end, McGwire was the first to surpass the record, finishing with a whopping 70 home runs for the season, while Sosa clubbed a grand total of 66. McGwire hit his 62nd home run in a game against the Cubs, and Sosa greeted him as he rounded the bases. But as he congratulated his colleague on breaking the long-held record, Sosa knew he had more to work for. "Right now I am going to keep continuing to do my job," he said. "Right now, I'm thinking about going to the playoffs."

The heroics displayed by Sosa, Wood, and 19-game winner Kevin Tapani earned the Cubs a 90–73 record and a playoff berth as a Wild Card team after beating the Giants in a special one-game playoff.

CENTER FIELDER · **HACK WILSON**

Standing only 5-foot-6, Lewis Wilson did not look the part of a major-league baseball player. His nickname, "Hack," is said to have had its origins in his resemblance to a professional wrestler named George Hackenschmidt. Wilson and his Cubs career were both short and intense. With a free-swinging style, the muscular outfielder terrorized pitchers for six seasons in a Chicago uniform. In 1930, he put together one of the best offensive seasons the game has ever seen, hitting .356 with 56 home runs and 191 RBI. That incredible RBI total remained a big-league record as of 2010.

HACK WILSON
CENTER FIELDER

CHICAGO
CUBS

STATS

Cubs seasons: 1926–31

Height: 5-foot-6

Weight: 190

- .307 career BA

- 4-time NL leader in HR

- 1,063 career RBI

- Baseball Hall of Fame inductee (1979)

Unfortunately, the Cubs came up short once again on the postseason stage, losing to the Atlanta Braves in three straight games in the NL Division Series (NLDS).

The new millennium began with another subpar season on Chicago's north side, but the Cubs turned things back around in 2001. Although the team's 88–74 record wasn't good enough to make the playoffs, right-handed starter Jon Lieber earned a trip to the 2001 All-Star Game by winning 20 games, and Wood continued to baffle hitters, striking out 217. It was enough to fan the flames of hope at Wrigley Field.

SO CLOSE . . . AGAIN

nder the leadership of new manager Dusty Baker, and with the help of pitcher Mark Prior, the team posted another 88–74 mark in 2003 and found itself on top of the realigned NL Central Division. Once again, Chicago faced Atlanta in the NLDS. This time, the Cubs beat the Braves three games to two to move on to the NLCS against the Florida Marlins. Chicago won three of the first five games, which sent the series

to Wrigley Field with the Cubs needing only one victory to get back to the World Series for the first time since 1945.

In Game 6, the Cubs were up 3–0 with one out in the eighth inning when disaster struck. Marlins second baseman Luis Castillo popped a foul ball toward the left-field stands that would almost certainly have been caught had a fan not interfered. Then the Cubs' usually sure-handed shortstop, Alex Gonzalez, booted a grounder that could have started an easy double play. Before the Cubs could escape from the

THE VOICE OF A LEGEND

Perhaps nothing calls to mind a Chicago Cubs game more vividly than the image of Harry Caray leaning out from his television broadcast booth and waving his microphone at the crowd as he led it in a rendition of "Take Me Out to the Ballgame" during the seventh inning stretch at Wrigley Field. Caray began his career as a broadcaster for the St. Louis Cardinals in 1945 but became a legend as the voice of the Cubs from 1982 to 1997. Known for his jovial spirit, Caray embodied the attitude of the "bleacher bums" in Wrigley, those blue-collar, fun-loving fans who made the outfield seats a constant good-natured party. That spirit earned him the

nickname, "The Mayor of Rush Street," a reference to a particularly festive part of Chicago. Caray's broadcasting mannerisms have been widely parodied and copied by broadcasters and comedians alike. A particular favorite of fans was his tendency to mispronounce players' names and sometimes even get them backwards! His trademark phrase, "Holy cow!" put an exclamation point on many great and not-so-great plays by the Cubs during his 16 years as Chicago's broadcaster. And when the home team would come out on top, fans couldn't wait to hear his favorite words: "Cubs win! Cubs win!"

RIGHT FIELDER · SAMMY SOSA

Sammy Sosa's career in a Cubs uniform was a roller-coaster ride of emotions for both the right fielder and the Chicago faithful. Beginning in 1995, "Slammin' Sammy" posted 9 consecutive seasons with more than 30 home runs and 100 RBI. He went on to become one of the most prolific home run hitters of all time, and in 1998, he and St. Louis Cardinals first baseman Mark McGwire engaged in an unforgettable race to eclipse baseball's hallowed single-season home run record. Relations between the slugger and Cubs officials soured in 2004, leading to his departure.

STATS

Cubs seasons: 1992–2004

Height: 6 feet

Weight: 220

- 609 career HR

- 1998 NL MVP

- 7-time All-Star

- 2-time NL leader in RBI

SAMMY SOSA
RIGHT FIELDER

CHICAGO
CUBS

MANAGER · FRANK CHANCE

Frank Chance was a solid-hitting first baseman for the Cubs from 1898 to 1912. In the middle of the 1905 season, Chance took over as player/manager for the team at the tender age of 27. During his tenure as manager, the Cubs never fell below third place in the NL and 4 times finished with more than 100 victories in a season. Nicknamed "The Peerless Leader," Chance led the Cubs to pennants in 1906, 1907, 1908, and 1910. He managed the way he played, with a hard-nosed, no-nonsense style that players respected. Under their Peerless Leader, the Cubs won the World Series in 1907 and 1908.

STATS

Cubs seasons as manager: 1905–12

Managerial record: 946–648

World Series championships: 1907, 1908

Baseball Hall of Fame inductee (1946)

FRANK CHANCE
MANAGER

CHICAGO
CUBS

nightmarish inning, the Marlins had scored eight runs and taken an insurmountable lead. Florida went on to defeat the reeling Cubs in Game 7. "It has nothing to do with the curse," Baker was quick to retort. "It has to do with fan interference and a very uncharacteristic error."

Instead of dwelling on the continuation of the curse, the Cubs put their energy into capturing that long-elusive pennant. The team signed slugging first baseman Derrek Lee in 2004 and brought back future Hall of Fame pitcher Greg Maddux, who had spent seven fine seasons with the club in the late 1980s and early '90s. Maddux capped his distinguished career by recording his 300th win on August 7, 2004. Still, the team failed to return to the playoffs in either 2004 or 2005.

The Cubs hit rock bottom in 2006, posting a miserable 66–96 record. The only bright spot in that dismal season was pitcher Carlos Zambrano, who notched 16 wins. Baker was fired and replaced by Lou Piniella, a veteran manager whose teams had won a combined total of more than 1,500 games at that time. Then came the signing of Alfonso Soriano, a speedy outfielder with uncommon home run power.

Despite those changes, the 2007 season started so poorly that Lee convened his teammates for a meeting during Memorial Day weekend to inspire a turnaround. "We're grown men, we're major-leaguers, we have to figure out a way to do our jobs better," Lee told reporters afterwards. "Right now it's embarrassing." His pep talk seemed to do the trick; by September 28, the team had clinched the NL Central title. Although the Cubs were swept by the Arizona Diamondbacks in the NLDS, it was clear that Chicago was back in contention.

Chicago's 2008 season confirmed that. The Cubs won 97 games, including the 10,000th victory in franchise history. Chicago sent an NL-record eight players to the All-Star game, including rookie catcher Geovany Soto. Zambrano was an All-Star as well, but his biggest moment came on September 14, when he threw the Cubs' first no-hitter since 1972.

After such a remarkable regular season, fans were hoping for an equally spectacular postseason. But the Cubs, who made it to

MARK PRIOR

THE CURSED CUBS

As of 2010, the last time the Chicago Cubs had played in the World Series was 1945. That's when team owner Phil Wrigley kicked Billy Sianis and his goat out of the park because he didn't like the goat's smell. A bitter Sianis, who had paid $7.50 for his goat's ticket, yelled, "The Cubs ain't gonna win no more!" That curse has been invoked every time the Cubs seem headed toward a championship season. In August 1969, the Cubs held a nine-game lead in the NL East when a black cat walked in front of their dugout during a game against the New York Mets. Chicago lost that game and so many more that it finished eight games back. In 2003, the team made it to the NLCS and held a three-games-to-two series lead over the Florida Marlins before the curse seemed to work its dark magic. During the eighth inning of Game 6, a fan reached for a foul ball just as Cubs left fielder Moises Alou was about to catch it. That missed out flustered the Cubs and gave the Marlins the momentum they needed to come back and win the series. "I don't think the curse is ever going to be broken," said Sam Sianis, Billy Sianis's nephew, in 2003.

ARAMIS RAMIREZ

Combining power with a keen batting eye, Cubs third baseman Aramis Ramirez averaged an outstanding 105 RBI a season from 2003 to 2008.

Despite the efforts of such veterans as Kosuke Fukudome (below) and Carlos Zambrano (opposite), the Cubs finished 2010 in the NL Central cellar.

KOSUKE FUKUDOME

the playoffs for the 16th time in their 132-year history, were once again stopped in the division series, this time by the Los Angeles Dodgers. They didn't get another chance in 2009 or 2010, missing the postseason both years. Although Piniella retired as manager late in the 2010 season, the emergence of hustling second baseman Ryan Theriot, steady-hitting shortstop Starlin Castro, and strong-armed outfielder Kosuke Fukudome gave Chicago fans hope that their Cubs would remain in the hunt.

Few teams in any sport can boast the kind of history and tradition the Chicago Cubs have built. Fewer still can claim the kind of loyalty and affection that the Cubs have received from their many fans over the years, even while enduring what is today baseball's longest World Series drought. As the wind from Lake Michigan blows another spring into Chicago each year, it brings with it the possibility that this—finally—will be the year the Cubs win it all.

INDEX